What Do You Want to Do?

Published in the UK by Scholastic Education, 2023
Scholastic Distribution Centre, Bosworth Avenue, Tournament Fields, Warwick, CV34 6UQ
Scholastic Ireland, 89E Lagan Road, Dublin Industrial Estate, Glasnevin, Dublin, D11 HP5F

SCHOLASTIC and associated logos are trademarks and/or registered trademarks of Scholastic Inc.
www.scholastic.co.uk
© 2023 Scholastic
1 2 3 4 5 6 7 8 9   3 4 5 6 7 8 9 0 1 2

Printed by Ashford Colour Press
The book is made of materials from well-managed, FSC®-certified forests and other controlled sources.

A CIP catalogue record for this book is available from the British Library.
ISBN 978-0702-32113-9

All rights reserved. This book is sold subject to the condition that it shall not, by way of trade or otherwise, be lent, hired out or otherwise circulated in any form of binding or cover other than that in which it is published. No part of this publication may be reproduced, stored in a retrieval system, or transmitted in any form or by any other means (electronic, mechanical, photocopying, recording or otherwise) without prior written permission of Scholastic.

Every effort has been made to trace copyright holders for the works reproduced in this publication, and the publishers apologise for any inadvertent omissions.

Author
Alice Hemming

Editorial team
Rachel Morgan, Vicki Yates, Fiona Undrill, Jennie Clifford

Design team
Dipa Mistry, Andrea Lewis, We Are Grace

Photographs
Cover gece33/iStock
p1, 4, 9 (cricket), 21 wavebreakmedia/Shutterstock
p5 (cricket) Mandy Kock/iStock
p5 (computer) Lucas Seijo/iStock
p5 (farming) Ian_Sherriffs/Shutterstock
p6 Monkey Business Images/Shutterstock
p7, 24 SolStock/iStock
p8 (basketball) simonkr/iStock
p8 (football) peepo/iStock
p9 (tennis) yacobchuk/iStock
p10 Ingrid Balabanova/Shutterstock
p11 Olena Yakobchuk/Shutterstock
p12–13 Norenko Andrey/Shutterstock
p14 Motortion Films/Shutterstock
p15, 24 Prostock-studio/Shutterstock
p3, 16 Jacob Lund/Shutterstock
p17 DC Studio/Shutterstock
p18 DEBOVE SOPHIE/iStock
p19 PeopleImages.com - Yuri A/Shutterstock
p20, 24 chuckmoser/iStock
p22–23 Pixel-Shot/iStock

Help your child to read!

This book practises these letters and letter sounds.
Point and say the sounds with your child:

- or (as in 'work')
- oul (as in 'could')
- au (as in 'sauces')
- oor (as in 'outdoors')
- tch (as in 'watch')
- al (as in 'calf')
- a (as in 'what')
- ear (as in 'earn')
- wr (as in 'write')
- sc (as in 'science')
- ch (as in 'school')
- ch (as in 'chef')

Your child may need help to read these common tricky words:

- do
- to
- are
- of
- they
- the
- anything
- thoughts
- many
- people
- one
- friends

Before reading
- Look at the cover picture and read the title together. Read the back cover blurb to your child.
- Ask your child: *What do you want to do when you grow up and leave school?*
- Talk about the image in the magnifying glass.

During reading
- If your child gets stuck on a word, remind them to sound it out and then blend the sounds to read the word: w-or-k, work.
- If they are still stuck, show them how to read the word.
- Enjoy looking at the pictures together. Pause to talk about the information.

After reading
- Talk about the images on page 24. What can your child tell you about them?
- Ask your child: *Which job in the book did you think looked the most interesting?*
- Talk to your child about different jobs they've heard about.

What do you want to do when you leave school?

There are hundreds of jobs. Let's research what you could do.

Teachers help children learn. Mostly, they work in schools. They love to watch children make progress.

A teacher gives a science lesson.

If you have talent and train hard, you could earn money playing sport.

football

basketball

If you don't make it to the top, you can still play matches after work.

tennis

cricket

Authors write books, magazine articles, websites – anything with words!

Authors are always writing down thoughts. They can switch between writing at home to writing in coffee shops, or even writing outdoors!

Chefs work in teams in hectic kitchens. It can be hot as chefs rush to cook the food and sauces. Chefs must learn to stay calm.

They take care to create delightful meals.

If you love animals and enjoy science at school, you could become a vet.

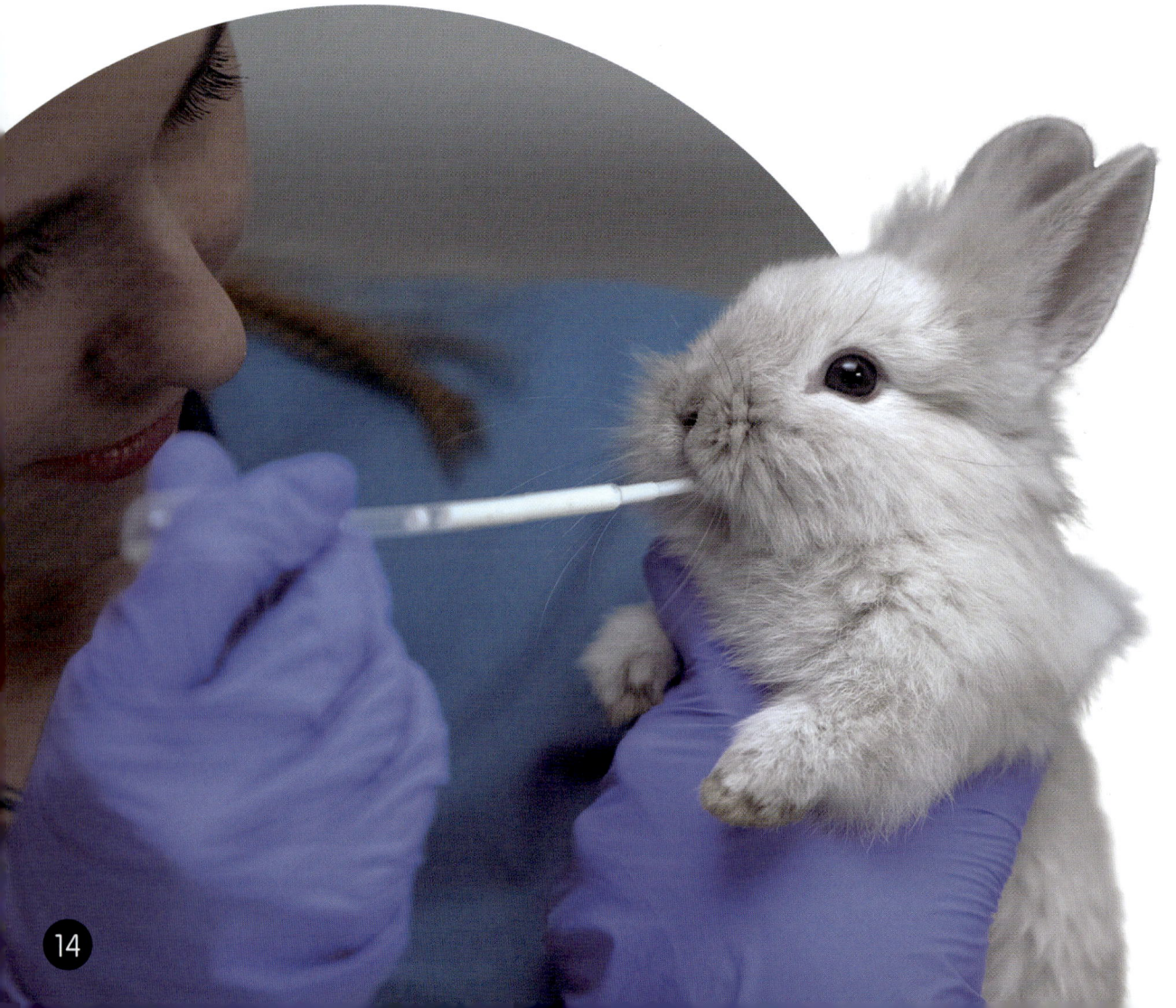

Vets search for the cause of an animal's sickness, then work out how to make them well.

Have you heard you can make money playing video games? It takes a lot of work but is fun.

You need to be good at computer science to become a games developer.

Farmers get up early and work outdoors in all weather, but many still say it is the best job in the world.

Some farmers grow crops and others raise animals.

farmer with a calf

Firefighters should be fit, good with people and able to stay calm.

Firefighters help in emergencies, like road accidents, as well as fires. They work to prevent fires, too.

visiting a school

Do you want a calm job or a lively one? Indoors or outdoors? Art or science? Talk about it with friends.
You have lots of time to decide!

They want to be chefs!

Talk about it!